MW01248362

Thoughts
from A-Z
FOR YOUR DAILY WALK

Edna Gray Jamison

Unless otherwise indicated, all scripture quotations are taken from the *King James Version* of the Bible. Public Domain.

Copyright © 2025 Edna Gray Jamison
ISBN: 979-8-9918826-1-3
All rights reserved.

Special Thanks

I would like to give special thanks to my pioneering mother, Missionary Edna Gray. She was a trailblazer and a lover of holiness. Everywhere she went she was literally a witness of the power of God. Her life changed when she said "yes" to Jesus in Miami, Florida. She surrendered her life so that she could live again. Her desire was to teach others that God was able to change their lives. Her ministry was a testimony that continues to live on in spiritual sons and daughters…of which, I am one.

"May I leave a deposit in the earth that will resonate and reverberate for decades to come."
- **Edna Gray Jamison**

Table of Contents

How To Use This Devotional

This devotional is a simple tool for individual or group study. There are many other encouraging words that can be associated with each letter of the alphabet. As you use this devotional, feel free to expand your devotional time by digging deeper in the passages of scriptures, prayers and thoughts to ponder.

POINT: This section outlines the focus of the specific day's devotion.

PASSAGES: Here you will find scriptures that support the devotional topic. You are encouraged to find other supportive scriptures as part of the Ponder section.

PRAYER: This section will be a prayer shared by the author to be a catalyst to help you pray the Word of God from the Devotional.

PONDER: Use this area to write out your thoughts, impressions and what you glean from the daily devotion that you should activate in your life.

ACKNOWLEDGE THE ANOINTING

POINT:
We acknowledge the truth of the Word of God by accepting that He has good in store for us. This creates a certainty that we then become recipients of the anointing. The anointing flows as we apply ourselves to hearing and doing the Word.

PASSAGES:
Isa 10:27 KJV
27 And it shall come to pass in that day, [that] his burden shall be taken away from off thy shoulder, and his yoke from off thy neck, and the yoke shall be destroyed because of the anointing.

Phm 1:6 NKJV
6 that the sharing of your faith may become effective by the acknowledgment of every good thing which is in you in Christ Jesus.

1Jo 2:27 KJV
27 But the anointing which ye have received of him abideth in you, and ye need not that any man teach you: but as the same anointing teacheth you of all things, and is truth, and is no lie, and even as it hath taught you, ye shall abide in him.

PRAYER:
Father, sometimes I struggle to believe that You have good plans and thoughts for me along with good

things for me. I do believe Your Word. I believe that Your Word is true and that it is truth for me.

Isaiah 10:27 says that the yoke (that thing, person or situation that holds me hostage) shall be destroyed because of the anointing. I receive Your anointing to be set free from every stronghold.

Today, I am open to the truth that as I acknowledge and accept as truth everything Your Word promised to me, that my faith and anointing increases. Above what I can see, hear or feel, I rest in Your promise.

PONDER:
In what ways has God's anointing removed burdens from your life?

_____

_____

_____

_____

_____

_____

_____

_____

BALANCE

POINT:
We are bombarded with so much that we can possibly focus on one area above all other areas. Some people prioritize bodily exercise to the degree that they discard all other areas. We find what appears to be fulfillment and satisfaction in life. However, Your Word says that bodily exercise PROFITS...but godliness is BENEFICIAL in every way. This truth brings balance to my life.

PASSAGES:
1Tim 4:8 KJV
For bodily exercise profiteth little: but godliness is profitable unto all things, having promise of the life that now is, and of that which is to come.

1 Tim 4:8 CSB
For the training of the body has limited benefit, but godliness is beneficial in every way, since it holds promise for the present life and also for the life to come.

PRAYER:
Father, when it feels like my world is upside down and seems impossible to maintain clarity, help me to run to You for balance. I understand that everything You made is good. When I am drawn to the busyness of life first and become overwhelmed, help me to recognize this imbalance and refocus on being the godly child that I am.

I understand that my health and physical well-being are significant to You. I also understand that my honoring and acknowledging You matters more.

Today, I rest in knowing that making You the Center of my life brings balance in every area of my life.

PONDER:
How can you better balance your spiritual, physical, and emotional well-being?

CALLED AND CHOSEN

POINT:
Many are called and few are chosen. I accept that I have been called and chosen by the Lord. I am confident in this because He called and chose me. I am accepted in Him. As people search for where they fit, I rest in knowing that I belong to and in Him.

PASSAGES:
1Co 1:9 KJV
9 God [is] faithful, by whom ye were called unto the fellowship of his Son Jesus Christ our Lord.

Rom 1:7 KJV
7 To all that be in Rome, beloved of God, called [to be] saints: Grace to you and peace from God our Father, and the Lord Jesus Christ.

1Co 1:2-3 KJV
2 Unto the church of God which is at Corinth, to them that are sanctified in Christ Jesus, called [to be] saints, with all that in every place call upon the name of Jesus Christ our Lord, both theirs and ours:
3 Grace [be] unto you, and peace, from God our Father, and [from] the Lord Jesus Christ.

PRAYER:
Father, it is with great joy that I read Your word knowing that I have been set apart for Your purpose and will. I no longer need to search for a place. I have found a place in You. Thank you for giving me comfort and confidence in the relationship that I have

in You. I remain grateful for all of the benefits that are provided through our relationship.

PONDER:
What does being *"called and chosen"* by God mean to you personally, and how can you live that out daily?

_____

_____

_____

_____

_____

_____

_____

_____

_____

_____

_____

_____

_____

_____

DEVOTION

POINT:
Devotion begins with our love for God and His Word. My commitment leads me to a deeper walk with God. Through my devotion, commitment and loyalty, I learn more about God, His ways and His plans for me.

PASSAGES:
Proverbs 16:3 KJV
Commit thy works unto the LORD, and thy thoughts shall be established.

Psa 37:4 KJV
Delight thyself also in the LORD; and he shall give thee the desires of thine heart.

Psa 37:23 KJV
The steps of a [good] man are ordered by the LORD: and he delighteth in his way.

Isa 58:14 KJV
Then shalt thou delight thyself in the LORD; and I will cause thee to ride upon the high places of the earth, and feed thee with the heritage of Jacob thy father: for the mouth of the LORD hath spoken [it].

PRAYER:
Dear Lord, when things are difficult and my devotion wanes, remind me that I am truly devoted to You, and You are devoted to me. Our relationship is one of commitment and loyalty. I learn to delight myself in You and You direct my thoughts. Father, help me to

delight myself in You and trust that my steps are being ordered.

PONDER:
How can you deepen your daily devotion time with God this week?

_____

_____

_____

_____

_____

_____

_____

_____

_____

_____

_____

_____

_____

$\mathcal{E}$XCELLENT

POINT:
Oh! Lord! Oh! Lord! How excellent is Your name! You are excellent! Your name is excellent! I declare that there is no One like You. You are altogether lovely. You are great. I am grateful for all that You provide in Your excellence!

PASSAGES:
Psa 8:9 KJV
O LORD our Lord, how excellent [is] thy name in all the earth!

Psa 36:7 KJV
How excellent [is] thy lovingkindness, O God! therefore the children of men put their trust under the shadow of thy wings.

Psa 148:13 KJV
Let them praise the name of the LORD: for his name alone is excellent; his glory [is] above the earth and heaven.

Psa 150:2 KJV
Praise him for his mighty acts: praise him according to his excellent greatness.

PRAYER:
Dear excellent Lord, as this day begins, help me to rely on Your excellent name and trust Your lovingkindness toward me.

PONDER:
What aspects of God's excellence have you experienced recently, and how can you praise Him for them?

_____

_____

_____

_____

_____

_____

_____

_____

_____

_____

_____

_____

_____

_____

$\mathcal{F}$EARLESS

POINT:
The chaos and confusion in this world, if allowed, would create an atmosphere of fear that is unrelenting. I am confident that my steps have been ordered and because of that, I do not live a life filled with anxiety, timidity or fear. I do not fear what is to come or what is not to come. My nature has changed since I began this journey to a new life. By staying in His face, I remain confident and fearless.

PASSAGES:
Pro 16:9 KJV
A man's heart deviseth his way: but the LORD directeth his steps.

2 Tim. 1:7 KJV
For God hath not given us the spirit of fear; but of power, and of love, and of a sound mind.

2 Tim. 1:7 NASB
For God has not given us a spirit of timidity, but of power and love and discipline.

2 Tim. 1:7 AMP
For God did not give us a spirit of timidity or cowardice or fear, but [He has given us a spirit] of power and of love and of sound judgment and personal discipline [abilities that result in a calm, well-balanced mind and self-control].

PRAYER:
Great God, help me to focus daily on You and Your promises instead of what I see, hear and feel. You are

truly greater than anything and anyone. You are
changing me into a fearless, confident servant. Amen.

PONDER:
What fears are holding you back, and how can faith
help you move forward courageously?

_____
_____
_____
_____
_____
_____
_____
_____
_____
_____
_____
_____
_____
_____

Goodness

POINT:
Your Word declares that You are good. It also reiterates that there is goodness following me all the days of my life. When I verbalize Psalm 23:6a, I smile.

PASSAGES:
Psa 23:6 KJV
Surely goodness and mercy shall follow me all the days of my life: and I will dwell in the house of the LORD forever.

Nahum 1:7 NIV
The Lord is good, a refuge in times of trouble. He cares for those who trust in him.

Psalm 31:19 NLT
How great is the goodness you have stored up for those who fear you. You lavish it on those who come to you for protection, blessing them before the watching world.

PRAYER:
Good God, as I recall all that You have provided and will provide, I lift my voice to declare that You are good! Thank You for being good to me. I will tell others about Your goodness and how You cover and protect them as they trust You.

PONDER:
How has God's goodness followed you this month, and how can you share that testimony with others?

UMILITY

POINT:
The way to go up is down in humility. As your child, my posture is down in prayer on my knees. Recognizing Your greatness causes me to maintain a heart of humility. You are my sufficiency wherever I lack, wherever I have need and whenever I feel inferior. My posture forever is humility.

PASSAGES:
2 Chron 7:14 AMP
and My people, who are called by My Name, humble themselves, and pray and seek (crave, require as a necessity) My face and turn from their wicked ways, then I will hear [them] from heaven, and forgive their sin and heal their land.

Psa 149:4 AMP
For the LORD takes pleasure in His people; He will beautify the humble with salvation.

Pro 11:2 AMP
When pride comes [boiling up with an arrogant attitude of self-importance], then come dishonor and shame, But with the humble [the teachable who have been chiseled by trial and who have learned to walk humbly with God] there is wisdom and soundness of mind.

Pro 29:23 AMP
A man's pride and sense of self-importance will bring him down, But he who has a humble spirit will obtain honor.

Jas 4:10 AMP
Humble yourselves [with an attitude of repentance and insignificance] in the presence of the Lord, and He will exalt you [He will lift you up, He will give you purpose].

1Pe 5:6 AMP
Therefore, humble yourselves under the mighty hand of God [set aside self-righteous pride], so that He may exalt you [to a place of honor in His service] at the appropriate time.

PRAYER:
Father, Your Word provides promises to those who walk humbly before You and whose hearts are humble toward You. I ask you, in the mighty Name of Jesus, to help me to walk humbly before You. I trust Your Word that You will lift me up and give me purpose. In the matchless Name of Jesus.

PONDER:
In what ways can you posture yourself more humbly before God today?

$\mathcal{I}$NCLINE

POINT:
I intentionally incline my ears and heart to God. Just as Jesus wanted Martha to incline herself to Him alongside her sister, Mary, Jesus wants us to incline our ears and hearts to hear His voice. He is always longing to speak to us; through us and in us.

PASSAGES:
Jos 24:23 KJV
Now therefore put away, [said he], the strange gods which [are] among you, and incline your heart unto the LORD God of Israel.

Psa 78:1 KJV [Maschil of Asaph]
Give ear, O my people, [to] my law: incline your ears to the words of my mouth.

Psa 141:4 KJV
Incline not my heart to [any] evil thing, to practise wicked works with men that work iniquity: and let me not eat of their dainties.

Isa 37:17 KJV
Incline thine ear, O LORD, and hear; open thine eyes, O LORD, and see: and hear all the words of Sennacherib, which hath sent to reproach the living God.

PRAYER:
Father, as I incline my ears to hear Your voice, it brings clarity and direction where needed. You are the Potter, and I am the clay. I submit to Your working in

me all that You desire as I incline my total being to You.

PONDER:
What distractions do you need to silence so you can better incline your heart and ears to God?

_____

_____

_____

_____

_____

_____

_____

_____

_____

_____

_____

_____

_____

JOY

POINT:
Jesus brings joy to life through our relationship and fellowship with Him. We should share the joy of our relationship with others so that they, too, can have this same peace and joy. The strength that we receive through the joy of our relationship with Jesus is a promise. God keeps His promise.

PASSAGES:
Neh 8:10 KJV
*Then he said unto them, Go your way, eat the fat, and drink the sweet, and send portions unto them for whom nothing is prepared: for [this] day [is] holy unto our Lord: neither be ye sorry; **for the joy of the LORD is your strength***.

Rom 15:13 ESV
May the God of hope fill you with all joy and peace in believing, so that by the power of the Holy Spirit you may abound in hope.

Psalm 16:11 ESV
You make known to me the path of life; in your presence there is fullness of joy; at your right hand are pleasures forevermore.

1Pe 1:8 KJV
Whom having not seen, ye love; in whom, though now ye see [him] not, yet believing, ye rejoice with joy unspeakable and full of glory:

PRAYER:
Father, in the midst of all that is happening in this life, I find unspeakable joy in knowing that You alone are my Strength. Today, I receive that joy and strength, in the mighty matchless name of Jesus.

PONDER:
What does "the joy of the Lord" mean to you right now, and how can you let it be your strength?

_____
_____
_____
_____
_____
_____
_____
_____
_____
_____
_____
_____

KNOW

POINT:
To know is to have certainty and confidence toward a situation, person or thing. It suggests a depth of intimacy. Jesus came as the Means for us to know our Father. We should make every effort to know God. The only way to know God is by knowing the Word of God; having certainty and confidence toward Him, His Word and His plan.

PASSAGES:
Rom 8:28 KJV
And we know that all things work together for good to them that love God, to them who are the called according to [his] purpose.

Dan 11:32 KJV
… but the people that do know their God shall be strong, and do [exploits].

Dan 11:32 NASB20
…but the people who know their God will be strong and take action.

PRAYER:
Father, there is such joy in having confidence in Your word and all that it provides and promises. You gave us Your word so that we could receive light and walk on the path of light to fulfill Your plan and will. I ask that You guide me continuously with confidence and certainty.

PONDER:
What truth about God do you *know* without a doubt, and how does that shape your choices?

_____

_____

_____

_____

_____

_____

_____

_____

_____

_____

_____

_____

_____

LIBERTY

POINT:
As blood bought believers, we have been given liberty through Jesus Christ! This liberty empowers us to live free from the power of sin and shame. We are encouraged to receive the truth that continues to free us to walk in liberty. How great it is to rest in the certainty of freedom in this life to let the weights of sin be lifted from our lives.

PASSAGES:
Gal 5:1 ESV
For freedom Christ has set us free; stand firm therefore, and do not submit again to a yoke of slavery.

John 8:36 ESV
So if the Son sets you free, you will be free indeed.

2 Cor 3:17 ESV
Now the Lord is the Spirit, and where the Spirit of the Lord is, there is freedom.

John 8:32 ESV
And you will know the truth, and the truth will set you free."

Isaiah 61:1 ESV
The Spirit of the Lord God is upon me, because the Lord has anointed me to bring good news to the poor; he has sent me to bind up the brokenhearted, to proclaim

liberty to the captives, and the opening of the prison to those who are bound;

Rom 8:1-2 LSB
There is therefore now no condemnation for those who are in Christ Jesus. For the law of the Spirit of life has set you free in Christ Jesus from the law of sin and death.

PRAYER:
Father, we love the truth that we find in Your Word. This truth makes us free from the power and penalty of sin. Thank you for setting me free through the power and truth in Your word. In the wonderful, liberating Name of Jesus, I am grateful!

PONDER:
Where do you need to fully embrace the liberty Christ has already given you?

_____

_____

_____

_____

_____

_____

_____

MEDITATE

POINT:
Meditation in the Word of God is a continual process of reading and praying the Word and doing it all again until it becomes a part of me. When I meditate in Your Word, I find such a sweetness in life. The wellspring of joy rises and encourages my soul. I will meditate more and more to encounter that freshness.

PASSAGES:
Jos 1:8 KJV
This book of the law shall not depart out of thy mouth; but thou shalt meditate therein day and night, that thou mayest observe to do according to all that is written therein: for then thou shalt make thy way prosperous, and then thou shalt have good success.

Psa 104:34 KJV
My meditation of him shall be sweet: I will be glad in the LORD.

Rom 12:2 KJV
And be not conformed to this world: but be ye transformed by the renewing of your mind, that ye may prove what [is] that good, and acceptable, and perfect, will of God.

Psalm 119

PRAYER:
Sometimes my world seems to race all around, Father, slow me down that I may meditate in Your

word. There in Your Word, I find all I need for transformation. In relationship with You, I find the sweetness and strength for the day's journey. Amen.

PONDER:
What scripture will you commit to meditating on this week, and how will you let it shape your thinking?

_____

_____

_____

_____

_____

_____

_____

_____

_____

_____

_____

_____

_____

EW MERCIES

POINT:
Our God has ample mercy and compassion for us. I refuse to be consumed by the activities and events of each day. Sometimes, I feel overwhelmed. At those times, I recall Your provision of new mercies. Then, peace rushes in to save the day! I am new because You give brand new mercies each day!

PASSAGES:
Lam 3:22-23 KJV
22 *It is of the LORD'S mercies that we are not consumed, because his compassions fail not.*
23 *They are] new every morning: great [is] thy faithfulness.*

Lam 3:22-23 AMP
22 *It is because of the LORD'S loving kindnesses that we are not consumed, Because His [tender] compassions never fail.*
23 *They are new every morning; Great and beyond measure is Your faithfulness.*

PRAYER:
Dear Father, may I continue to understand and receive new unfathomable mercies each morning. Knowing that Your faithfulness is constant and unchanging, each day when I rise, I have renewed hope.

PONDER:
How have God's new mercies renewed your hope in a difficult season?

OCCUPY

POINT:
I have been called to occupy until the Lord returns. To occupy can be defined, in essence, as to carry on business or to busy oneself with a task. Seeing the destitution and deprivation of our world, I must focus on the tasks at hand that call me to serve the Lord in every way.

PASSAGES:
Luk 19:13 KJV
And he called his ten servants, and delivered them ten pounds, and said unto them, Occupy till I come.

PRAYER:
Father, as Your servant, I have received what I need to be busy serving faithfully until You return. When I grow weary, remind me that I must maintain confidence that You see me and desire me to utilize every gift that You've placed in me. Grateful. Thank You for helping me live in the best manner to occupy until Your return.

PONDER:
What assignment or area has God called you to "occupy" faithfully, and are you giving it your best?

_____

_____

_____

$\mathcal{P}$RIORITIES

POINT:
We prioritize what is valuable to us. My relationship with You is the highest priority and everything else revolves around You. No matter who else decides to set their priorities on something or someone else, my focus is clear. YOU.

PASSAGES:
Mat 6:33 KJV
33 But seek ye first the kingdom of God, and his righteousness; and all these things shall be added unto you.

Pro 3:6 KJV
6 In all thy ways acknowledge him, and he shall direct thy paths.

PRAYER:
Father, I ask for Your guidance to set priorities in life. I know that You see beyond this moment. My tomorrow is already seen by Your loving eyes. Help me to ask and receive directions in goal setting and prioritizing the ups and downs and the ins and outs of life. It is so.

PONDER:
What priorities do you need to shift to truly put God first?

QUIETNESS

POINT:
Sometimes the noise is so loud in the world and my head that it is almost deafening. When I learn to practice quietness, I gain strength that I didn't even know I possessed! This quietness produces the assurance, confidence and empowerment that I need to be the solid, victorious child that I have been called to be! Shhhh!! I am practicing quietness and rest for my confident victory.

PASSAGES:
Isa 30:15 KJV
15 For thus saith the Lord GOD, the Holy One of Israel; In returning and rest shall ye be saved; in quietness and in confidence shall be your strength: and ye would not.

Isa 32:17 KJV
17 And the work of righteousness shall be peace; and the effect of righteousness quietness and assurance forever.

PRAYER:
Father, I submit to the quietness that You promised to Your children. If I have learned the habit of always needing noise to bring fulfillment, today, I lay that aside and ask for Your quietness instead. It's in Your quietness that I receive all I need for success. Amen.

PONDER:
How can you create space today to hear God in the stillness?

RESTORATION

POINT:
The promise of restoration suggests that one initially possessed that thing in prime condition. We serve the God of restoration. He is able to make new what has been tarnished, blemished or stolen. As life can often take from us the joy and gleam of a thing, our God promises to restore joy, comfort, healing and complete recovery...just as if it never happened. However, we must be willing to release the past pain to receive the restored joy and peace.

PASSAGES:
Psa 51:12 KJV
12 Restore unto me the joy of thy salvation; and uphold me [with thy] free spirit.

Isa 57:18 KJV
18 I have seen his ways and will heal him: I will lead him also and restore comforts unto him and to his mourners.

Jer 30:17 KJV
17 For I will restore health unto thee, and I will heal thee of thy wounds, saith the LORD; because they called thee an Outcast, [saying], This [is] Zion, whom no man seeketh after.

Joe 2:25 KJV
25 And I will restore to you the years that the locust hath eaten, the cankerworm, and the caterpiller, and the palmerworm, my great army which I sent among you.

PRAYER:
Father, when my path seems dark and dismal, Your word provides illumination and light. Thank you for making promises to me. I am especially grateful for the promise of restoration. Even if I was a party to the destruction in my own life, I receive the restoring power through the power You give. I trust You to do what only You can do: restore the joy that comes from salvation. In the mighty and matchless name of Jesus.

PONDER:
What is God restoring in your life right now, and how can you partner with Him in that process?

_____

_____

_____

_____

_____

_____

_____

_____

_____

SANCTIFICATION

POINT:
Sanctification is a posture of the heart that overflows into the soul and every aspect of the life of the one who is sanctified. Humbling oneself before the Sanctifier is required before they can be sanctified or set apart for the purpose of the Sanctifier. Sanctification begins on the inside (heart) and then proceeds to the outside (the body and the world in which we interact).

PASSAGES:
Lev 20:7-8 KJV
7 Sanctify yourselves therefore and be ye holy: for I [am] the LORD your God.
8 And ye shall keep my statutes and do them: I [am] the LORD which sanctify you.

Eze 36:23 KJV
23 And I will sanctify my great name, which was profaned among the heathen, which ye have profaned in the midst of them; and the heathen shall know that I [am] the LORD, saith the Lord GOD, when I shall be sanctified in you before their eyes.

Jhn 17:17 KJV
17 Sanctify them through thy truth: thy word is truth.

1Th 5:23 KJV
23 And the very God of peace sanctify you wholly; and [I pray God] your whole spirit and soul and body be

preserved blameless unto the coming of our Lord Jesus Christ.

PRAYER:
Father, sanctify me completely body, soul and spirit. As I submit to Your sanctifying power, I receive all that You have purposed for me. Help me to live out Your will in this life in complete sanctification. Amen.

PONDER:
In what ways is God calling you to be set apart in this season?

_____

_____

_____

_____

_____

_____

_____

_____

_____

TRIUMPH

POINT:
Today I meditate on the triumphant victory that is mine. No matter what challenges come today, I am certain that God always cause me to overcome and be triumphant in that thing. Should I not succeed in that thing or situation, I know that God has a plan to get me to triumphant victory.

PASSAGES:
Psa 25:2 KJV
2 O my God, I trust in thee: let me not be ashamed, let not mine enemies' triumph over me.

Psa 41:11 KJV
11 By this I know that thou favourest me, because mine enemy doth not triumph over me.

[sa 92:4 KJV
4 For thou, LORD, hast made me glad through thy work: I will triumph in the works of thy hands.

2Co 2:14 KJV
14 Now thanks [be] unto God, which always causeth us to triumph in Christ, and maketh manifest the savour of his knowledge by us in every place.

PRAYER:
Father, thank you for the promise to not let me be ashamed because of my confident, reliance in You. Thank you for favor along with goodness and mercy

that continuously follow me all the days of my life.
Amen.

PONDER:
What past triumph can you remember today to fuel
your faith for present challenges?

_____

_____

_____

_____

_____

_____

_____

_____

_____

_____

_____

_____

_____

_____

$\mathcal{U}$NITY

POINT:
We are members of the family of God. We are brothers and sisters. There will be an opportunity for division, but we should all strive to keep the unity that comes from our ties with each other. The Spirit of God dwells in us. We are to obey the Word to live and walk in unity with each other as we continually grow in knowledge of the Word.

PASSAGES:
Psa 133:1 KJV
1 [A Song of degrees of David.] Behold, how good and how pleasant [it is] for brethren to dwell together in unity!

Eph 4:3, 13 KJV
3 Endeavoring to keep the unity of the Spirit in the bond of peace. ...
13 Till we all come in the unity of the faith, and of the knowledge of the Son of God, unto a perfect man, unto the measure of the stature of the fulness of Christ:

PRAYER:
Father, help me to be a unifying factor in the lives of others and in this world as You see fit. Help me to always stand for truth and right that brings liberty and freedom, and You will use me as needed to be a conduit for You.

PONDER:
How can you be a peacemaker and promote unity within your community or family?

_____

_____

_____

_____

_____

_____

_____

_____

_____

_____

_____

_____

_____

_____

VALOR

POINT:
Valor is thought to be having courage, strength of mind, all the while facing danger. Danger is all around us as we have an adversary who desires to steal, kill and destroy us. We are not fearful of the adversary who brings dangerous situations. We rest in knowing that just as God called Gideon and other mighty men of valor, we, too have been called to be your children of VALOR. We are fearless, filled with courage and strength.

PASSAGES:
Exo 15:2-3 KJV
2 The LORD [is] my strength and song, and he is become my salvation: he [is] my God, and I will prepare him an habitation; my father's God, and I will exalt him. 3 The LORD [is] a man of war: the LORD [is] his name.

Psa 18:29 KJV
29 For by thee I have run through a troop; and by my God have I leaped over a wall.

PRAYER:
Father, my DNA and expectations change as I read and believe what You say about me. You changed me from the fearful and afraid to the strong and valiant one that wholly trusts You. You are truly my Help! So, it is.

PONDER:
Where is God calling you to show courage and take a bold step of faith?

_____

_____

_____

_____

_____

_____

_____

_____

_____

_____

_____

_____

_____

_____

_____

WISDOM

POINT:
The Word of God encourages those who lack wisdom, to ask for it. Wisdom is knowing what to do and we have opportunity to ask for wisdom.

PASSAGES:
Pro 2:6 KJV
6 For the LORD giveth wisdom: out of his mouth [cometh] knowledge and understanding.

Jas 1:5 KJV
5 If any of you lack wisdom, let him ask of God, that giveth to all [men] liberally, and upbraideth not; and it shall be given him.

Psa 111:10 KJV
10 The fear of the LORD [is] the beginning of wisdom: a good understanding have all they that do [his commandments]: his praise endureth for ever.

PRAYER:
Great God, Who provides wisdom to all petitioners, give me wisdom! I honor and stand in awe of You. I am grateful for Your willingness to hear and answer my cry for wisdom. Thank you for the knowledge and understanding promised.

PONDER:
What area of your life do you need to seek God's wisdom?

E*X*ALT

POINT:
Magnifying You, Your name and Your mighty acts bring such clarity in the middle of every cloudy day. I am determined to exalt You despite what is happening in the world and my life. You deserve all of the honor and the glory.

PASSAGES:
Psa 30:1 NLT
1 A psalm of David. A song for the dedication of the Temple. I will exalt you, LORD, for you rescued me. You refused to let my enemies triumph over me.

Psa 145:1 KJV
1 [[David's [Psalm] of praise.]] I will extol thee, my God, O king; and I will bless thy name for ever and ever.

Psa 145:1 NLT
1 A psalm of praise of David. I will exalt you, my God and King, and praise your name forever and ever.

Isa 25:1 KJV
1 O LORD, thou [art] my God; I will exalt thee, I will praise thy name; for thou hast done wonderful [things; thy] counsels of old [are] faithfulness [and] truth.

PRAYER:
I exalt You for all that You have done for me. You are worthy to be magnified considering that my enemies were not allowed to triumph over me. You protected

and kept me! Thank you for your continued faithfulness. I will always eXalt Your name, Great God!

PONDER:
In what ways can you exalt God with your words and actions this week?

_____

_____

_____

_____

_____

_____

_____

_____

_____

_____

_____

_____

_____

_____

ƳIELD NOT
(TO TEMPTATION)

POINT:
Oh, for the blessing that comes from enduring temptation! It is certain that temptations and trials will come. God has made a way for us to escape and/or endure the temptation with a positive outcome.

PASSAGES:
Psa 119:11 KJV
11 Thy word have I hid in mine heart, that I might not sin against thee.

1 Co 10:13 KJV
13 There hath no temptation taken you but such as is common to man: but God [is] faithful, who will not suffer you to be tempted above that ye are able; but will with the temptation also make a way to escape, that ye may be able to bear [it].

Jas 1:12 KJV
12 Blessed [is] the man that endureth temptation: for when he is tried, he shall receive the crown of life, which the Lord hath promised to them that love him.

Mat 26:41 KJV
41 Watch and pray, that ye enter not into temptation: the spirit indeed [is] willing, but the flesh [is] weak.

Heb 4:16 KJV

16 Let us therefore come boldly unto the throne of grace, that we may obtain mercy, and find grace to help in time of need.

Mat 6:13 KJV
13 And lead us not into temptation but deliver us from evil: For thine is the kingdom, and the power, and the glory, forever. Amen.

PRAYER:
Father, I come with confidence and boldness to ask for the power to not yield to temptations. As the tests come, I realize that I am not the only one being tempted. I know that You provide a way for me to escape. If I have thoughts contrary to the Word, I bring them under the submission of the Word. Help me learn how to endure and fight from the vantage point of power and faith. Thank you for the promise!

PONDER:
What temptation do you need to resist today, and what escape route has God already provided?

ZACHARIAS

POINT:
Zacharias means that the Lord has remembered. As we look at the life of John, Jesus' cousin, we know the prophetic way that he came into the world. The angel told Zacharias that his prayers were heard. This means that God remembered him by answering his prayers. God hears us and before we even see the fulfillment, we must believe that God remembers and answers.

PASSAGES:
Luk 1:13 KJV
13 But the angel said unto him, Fear not, Zacharias: for thy prayer is heard; and thy wife Elisabeth shall bear thee a son, and thou shalt call his name John.

Gen 8:1 KJV
1 And God remembered Noah, and every living thing, and all the cattle that [was] with him in the ark: and God made a wind to pass over the earth, and the waters asswaged;

Gen 19:29 KJV
29 And it came to pass, when God destroyed the cities of the plain, that God remembered Abraham, and sent Lot out of the midst of the overthrow, when he overthrew the cities in the which Lot dwelt.

[Gen 30:22 KJV]
22 And God remembered Rachel, and God hearkened to her, and opened her womb.

PRAYER:
Father, when Your word says that You remember someone, it really means that You have or will take action on their behalf. Remember me and move on my behalf. Thank you for keeping me on Your mind.

PONDER:
What long-standing prayer are you still believing God to answer, trusting that He has remembered you?

_____

_____

_____

_____

_____

_____

_____

_____

_____

_____

_____

About the Author

While many chase titles, fortune and fame, she's crystal clear that her purpose is only defined by God. As a minister, psalmist, speaker and author, Edna Jamison knows that she is not only called to share the Gospel in a unique, authentic way—but she is also called to usher believers into the life of abundance, peace and prosperity that God promised in His Word. On a mission to help others find their unique purpose and passion, Edna is the walking epitome of Ephesians 2:10, empowering others, *"... to do good works, which God prepared in advance for us to do."*

Ministering in some form or fashion since she was a child, Edna is no stranger to the ministerial marketplace. Serving as the founder and leader of Graced for Today, Edna strategically shares Biblical revelations via live videos on Facebook, YouTube, Instagram and Twitter. After many requests for an extended Bible study, Edna soon created L.I.F.E. (Live In Faith Everyday) Bible class where she teaches Biblical principles on Zoom and Facebook one Saturday a month. Listeners and viewers of all backgrounds leave inspired and motivated through the light of the Word—better positioning them to believe both that they are who God says they are and that He will do what He promised.

In her debut book, *30 Lessons on Unapologetic Living: Living Life Without Regret*, she uses modern-day parables and stories from the Word of God to give readers simple truths they can apply to everyday fruitful living. Short, but powerful, these lessons on life, leadership and God's perfect love challenges readers to live a life of victory and strength in spite of their external circumstances. For readers of all ages and faith levels, *30 Lessons on*

Unapologetic Living Study Guide and Journal can be indulged in as a daily devotional or a periodic jolt of hope.

Her second book, "*What's Your Egypt?*", was released in December 2024. She is continually expanding her product line and offerings. Be on the lookout for more publications soon.

For speaking engagements or booking, visit www.gracedfortoday.org, email edna.jamison@gracedfortoday.org or call (601) 909-5580.

Made in the USA
Columbia, SC
10 July 2025

60272465R00037